FOREWARD

Prepare yourself for California during the gold rush, It's mid-Nineteenth Century and the living is rough and dangerous. A lot of men have come to the Promised Land for gold but the competition, the frenzy of dreams mixed with greed results, as is often the case when it comes to riches, in somebody gets dead pretty quick. Claims get jumped, gold carriers murdered, and if that's not enough, the weather can take you down.

The story is remarkable for its authenticity. Especially striking to me was the amazing command of diction, those words and phrases that colored the dialogue of the times but have largely been lost to generations that follow, a way of speaking among the characters that seems as if it was lifted right out of the Barbary Coast days. More truth in fiction, they say, than in some documentaries. You can learn a lot from this story especially since it is written by someone who has a rich, studied knowledge of the times.

What you will see in this book, in addition to an accurate portrayal of terrain, its conditions, and the human interactions of the times, is a compelling manifestation of the danger we all sense at the very beginning. In that way, among others, the story does not disappoint. Hold on to your hats!

David Watts
Best Selling Author of *The Guns of Pecos County* and *The Long Ride*

"Why does it always have to be you that goes?" said Elizabeth. "Its so dangerous."

They'd had this discussion before. Josh didn't look up from his packing to answer. If he'd done so, he'd be looking into his wife's relentless stare.

"Because it's dangerous, so it can't be anyone but me. It's our money and I can't trust someone else to protect it."

"There are people you trust. Why not ask them?"

"There are precious few I trust in gold country and those few have become friends. How can I ask a friend to take on something I wouldn't do myself?"

Elizabeth knew Josh was never one to shirk a dangerous prospect just as she knew he was right. He would leave her behind and go up country.

Josh and Elizabeth Bonner owned a piece of a very successful claim in the dry diggings near Hangtown, another small camp called Bright Hope and a piece of an operation they'd staked on Blue Lead Creek. Once every month or so the gold from the claims needed to be transported back to San Francisco where the dust and flakes could be extracted and refined into ingots of various denominations. The transfer was a dangerous operation. Bushwhackers and other desperadoes were a constant threat. Josh insisted on the undertaking himself, accompanied by two other men with similar paying stakes, a coach driver, and a guard.

They tried to vary the days of their departure so they did not congregate in public prior to leaving. As a first precaution Josh had purchased a small steam launch to cross the bay. All the brightwork including the boiler had been painted a flat black. Josh embarked silently on the flood tide. He drifted along, occasionally dipping an oar to keep course. He slipped past Washerwoman's Cove where several women were working under torchlight. None even looked up to note his passage. About a mile further was his rendezvous. Picking up two flashes from a shuttered lamp he pulled toward shore where the current released its hold. Another flash from the lamp and the voice of Garrett Thoms sounded from the reeds. No sooner had the keel bumped ground and Thoms tossed his gear aboard before he pushed the boat away, skillfully slipping over the bow. Another mile along and the signal and boarding were repeated. Zachary Hammel, older and not so spry, cursed loudly as he dragged both boots in the water before flopping over the gunwale. Once back in the current, Josh stoked the firebox. They would have a good head of steam by slack tide.

Any villain who wished them harm would have to ride around the entire bay to follow them. Once inside the estuary of the Sacramento River they would join up with their coach-and-four, hiding the launch under a tarp in the reeds. . The driver and shotgun rider were men the three stakeholders had confidence in. Besides, they outnumbered them three to two. While there was a chance of a random robbery the real danger would come on the return trip when the coach was laden with washed gold.

###

The launch was beached within a wide thicket of rushes. The trio walked upstream to the rendezvous by the stand of cottonwoods. Josh was last to board the coach, giving a nod to the driver and guard. He stepped around the flat, metal strongbox bolted to the floor, flopping down on the seat beside Garrett Thoms. Thoms had gold holdings but accumulated his wealth in lumber, a commodity on short commons in San Francisco.

Across from Josh and the aspiring lumber baron sat Zachary Hammel, a veteran of the mining camps who claimed he made his fortune one pan at a time. Perhaps that was so three years ago, but he quickly saw the advantage in supplying the miners instead of becoming one. In the army, he'd been a teamster so it was a natural transition. Hammel liked to dress the part and cultivated both the look and smell of the lone placer miner looking for a grubstake. He looked like he'd passed out in an alley but was welcome in what passed for parlor society in San Francisco. Taking a seat as far from Hammel in the coach was an easy choice.

Josh Bonner, Hammel, and Thoms weren't the richest men in the San Francisco but they were, by any standard, wealthy men. All three were taciturn by nature, a good thing. None were prone to small talk or frivolous conversations, at least when sober. The coach was just as noisy with the added discomfort of being tossed about like dice in a cup as the coach navigated the nearly non-existent trails between camps. The three would be battered and bounced for the four hours it would take to Sutter's Landing. There they would rest the horses and tend to their aches and bruises at the adobe-walled hacienda of Wilhelm Van Volk and his family. Josh had emigrated west from Missouri in 1848 with the Van Volks. The Dutch family now ran a successful bakery and eatery in the settlement above the landing. They built one of the first permanent homes in the gold country, set on the backside of the hill behind the Landing. The home was modeled on the haciendas of the Mexican land grant owners who had lorded over Alta

California before the *Californios* cast the *jefes* aside. The small plaza inside the adobe walls would afford the travelers and their horses a brief rest and the last decent meal they would enjoy for the week it would take to make the rounds of the camps.

The journey upriver as far as Sutter's was without much peril. The return trip, laden with riches was a different enterprise. They would be sitting ducks between the narrow banks and could be easily ambushed from men concealed in the grass and rushes on the shoreline or from the trees lining the road.

Sutter's Landing was one of the first places Josh and Elizabeth Bonner arrived in early December of 1848. The place hadn't changed appearance or purpose in the subsequent three years. The gravel and sand shoreline was stacked with trade goods and discarded wares. Small boats lie anchored or overturned on the beach. Some boats were propped on their sides with a small fire for warming the men who guarded the stacks of goods and slept under the boats when they could. From the beach the mud streets of the settlement carried to the top of a low hill. All the muck and refuse of daily commerce and human striving sluiced down to the shoal. A breeze off the distant ocean spared the party the worst of the stench. Even at this late hour, saloon tents were lit from the inside and the carousing of drunks, gamblers, and those who preyed on them wafted on the same wind.

The coach angled off away from the settlement and ascended the hill as they rounded it from the south. The banked embers of a few campfires marked where decent men encamped away from the squalor. Once the crest was behind them, lights from the Van Volk hacienda could be seen. They were a family of bakers and rose early. Josh stepped down at the gates to the compound, sucking in the fresh, unsullied air. Thanks to Hammel, the interior of the coach was reminiscent of the encampment behind them. The Van Volks, after all, were Josh's friends so it was customary he would be the one to knock. It was almost a ritual and part of the same dance, that Willie Van Volk would answer the knock and grip Josh in a heartfelt embrace. Together the two friends opened the gates. The coach rolled in and headed toward the horse barn.

Another old friend awaited Josh at the stables. Natchez, his sorrel stallion now resided with the Van Volks. The horse would not have survived San Francisco. He'd have died, been stolen, eaten, or all three. Here there was pasture, a stall, and good care. Natchez began nickering even before Josh entered the barn. The old friends greeted each other with the same gusto Josh and Willie had.

"I think you come here just to visit the horse, yes?" said Willie. "You come see the horse before you see Hannah and the girls."

"I feel and smell like a goat after traveling all night. I ain't nothin' they'd want to nuzzle up to."

"You clean up, then come to the house. Leave your friend here," he said, nodding toward Hammel. "He smells like he's been sleeping with a dead goat."

Josh chuckled. Hammel was the reason they slept and ate in the barn on their visits. Josh was, of course, treated like family and Thoms was decent company but Hammel could make your eyes water. They couldn't very well turn him out by himself so it was decided the monthly visitors would make do with a barn roof over their head and clean hay for a bed. Josh cleaned himself up best he could with a bucket of well water, then bunked into a stall to sleep. The household of a baker rose early and worked till the job was done. He didn't want to interrupt their routine as the women gushed over him, even if he did still smell like a goat.

Josh awoke to the aroma of cinnamon hot from the oven and coffee steaming in the pot. The Mexican cook set a covered woven basket and a speckled blue coffeepot down on the plank table. She pulled three matching mugs from the basket as Hammel's hacking voice called out.

"There better be some damn bacon on the table when I get there."

"*Si, senor*" said the cook, spitting into one of the cups before pouring steaming coffee into it. She gave Josh a conspiratorial look before setting that cup off to the side. The cook departed for her work at the bakery-café. In the basket Josh found pastries, meat, and vegetables wrapped in *tortillas*. Two of the wraps had a note sitting on them. "*Para el hombre sucio*", another gift for Hammel from the cook.

The family had already left to serve breakfast to the hungry residents of the landing. The coach was made ready and rolled out the gate with an extra horse tethered behind. Josh rode Natchez and thought about visiting the café but figured the Van Volks would be too busy. The party rejoined the road leading out of Sutter's, paralleling the river. Josh rode trail, keeping back a ways to watch for anyone taking a special interest in the coach's passage. Soon everyone was curious about the goings on in the coach.

Thoms leaned out the window and yelled to the driver, "Pull this damn thing over to the barber's tent there."

Once stopped Thoms burst out the door and bellowed, "Git your scrawny butt out of there, Hammel. If I have to come for you I'll yank your beard out and save the barber the trouble."

"I ain't gonna," said Hammel defiantly.

"You better be ready by the time I come back," warned Thoms as he stormed through the flaps of the tent. Josh caught up and peered inquisitively into the stage.

"Sum bitch thinks I'm too ripe for his fancy company. Says he'll throw me off if I don't get a bath, shave, and a haircut." Hammel was working himself up but he knew Thoms didn't make idle threats.

"I think its best. Hell, you been scratchin' your collection of nits and fleas since you got in the boat." The remark earned him a sour look from Hammel as he scratched at his beard, then realized what he was doing. He was stepping down when Thoms emerged from the tent.

"Cost me five dollars but it's worth it not to have to gag with every breath for the week. You strip out here. I'm gonna burn those rags before they run off by themselves and start a plague."

A crowd had gathered and laughed and chimed in with insults as the man peeled his clothes off until he was naked except for a cloth he held over his privates. He ducked into the tent and soon the filthy cloth came back out to the guffaws of the gathering. Thoms took Josh by the elbow and led him away.

"I promised I'd buy him new duds and rent him a whore when we get to Hangtown. Let's see what we can find."

"Glad it was you, not me, what broke him. That man's got a tough hide on him."

"That coating of filth is what passes for a tough hide. He's afraid of most folk and the stench keeps them away. I swear I've buried corpses smelled better'n that walkin' privy. He'll be meek as a mouse when we get back. Look, there's a place sellin' gum boots."

Zachary Hammel was still in the barber's chair when Thoms and Josh passed the still smoldering pile of rags and entered the barber's tent. Hammel's stench had been replaced by the eye-watering smell of the turpentine the man had been doused with to kill the vermin that called Zachary Hammel home. The barber was just finishing up shaving Hammel's dome, trying his damnedest to cover the turpentine odor with bay rum. Hammel reclined in the chair, scrubbed pink as a baby and just as happy. A comely Chinese girl was scrubbing at his nails.

"Hey gents, what do ya think?" Hammel was in a much better mood. Surely the half-empty glass of whiskey and the stone jug on the counter behind him had as much to do with his frame of mind as the ministering of the barber. Four other customers waited their turn or maybe they just came in for the show. Each of the men held whiskey glasses, courtesy of the patient's largesse. They were all old pals now.

"We got you new everything from belts to boots," said Thoms, holding up replacement items for Hammel's approval. Josh carried paper wrapped bundles of replacements for the replacements.

"All that new gear on I'll look like I ain't been in California but half an hour. How 'bout you run out and get me a pick and a pan to finish the show. But first let's have a drink."

Josh's experience with alcohol wasn't extensive and it didn't include clinking glasses two hours after sunup. In the spirit of the moment, Thoms lifted the jug on his arm and took a healthy pull. Josh made the same jug-over-arm drinking display but just wet his lips. He smacked them but discovered no one was paying him a lick of attention.

"Looks like a shave and a bath didn't kill you, Zach," said Thoms.

"Well, the day ain't done but I'll agree I don't mind being fussed over, especially by this sweet Celestial. She knows how to run a scrub brush and she don't take no sass. I'll pay you back the five dollars but you're still on the hook for the whore."

"Will be money well spent. Say goodbye to your bar buddies. Let's get on the trail." The two partners retired to the coach to wait for the newly minted miner.

"Zachary was wearing that layer of dirt and stink like a shield. He's by nature a loner. He figured keeping people at a distance kept them from getting to his gold. Now, I'm afraid we may have created a dandy. Don't think he'll ever fit in with society but I think he's found a home with the barbershop crowd."

Just then Hammel emerged from the tent in his new duds, stepping carefully to avoid the worst of the mud. When Hammel alighted the combination of turpentine, whiskey, and bay rum made their eyes water. Thoms may yet regret the money spent. Josh retreated—glad he drew the first stint trailing the coach. The two older men were treating each other like long lost brothers in contrast to the tense silence of last evening. It was a welcome change. He hoped it would last. The coach departed and Josh lingered until he figured they had a mile start on him. Natchez moved out with a gentle pressure from Josh's legs.

Despite marriage to a woman he loved and father to a child he adored, Josh Bonner was also of a solitary nature. The company of his fellows seemed always to lead to bickering and discord. The emigration from Missouri was a daily argument about every detail of every day's march. His months in the gold fields and in the aptly named Hangtown camp were a constant battle of wills with his fellow miners over shares, where to mine, who had what duty on any given day. There was no relief in the mining camp. Miners would go to the camp to blow off steam. They bore it with them to the makeshift bars. Unloading it on the man who spilled their drink with his elbow or a dispute would erupt between who was better at cards, women, mining, drinking, or shooting. The life of an Argonaut was hard enough without the burden of camp society. No wonder many prospectors preferred to pack their life on a mule and head up into the hills alone.

Josh might enjoy his meditative solitude but contemplation didn't mean he was any less aware of his surroundings. The trail paralleled the Sacramento River as it wound upstream to Sutter's Fort. The east bank was a mix of trees and open beaches. The western side was higher banked and almost wooded completely. Just outside of the landing was what passed as the local cemetery. Those with friends or those who died with money in their pockets and discovered before the corpse could be looted took up residence at the cemetery. Lumber was scarce as were stonemasons so few were interred in coffins. Fewer had headstones. Generally the departed were wrapped in a blanket. After burial a single carved plank would mark their final rest. Those who could afford the luxury had a rough granite boulder placed at the head with shallow chips removed to provide the relevant words and dates.

For those without friends or sufficient custom, burial meant a short boat ride across the river, being hoisted up the bank and deposited back in the woods. Payment for this service was typically set at salvage of the deceased belongings. Those with friends but no money insisted the service be carried out in daylight. A nighttime woods internment might never reach the far shore before the body was unceremoniously pitched overside with the pockets full of rocks for ballast.

While friends and acquaintances might mourn the loss of a companion and drink the appropriate number of toasts in their memory the prevailing philosophy was "dead is dead". Gold was the business of the new state and all the aspects of finding the color, extracting it, and safeguarding it were the order of the day. Anyone who wasn't actively seeking gold was in the business of providing equipment, food, housing, or entertainment for those who did. Little else mattered. None came to build schools or churches or civic buildings. No one surveyed streets beyond pacing off enough land to drive stakes in the corners and offer it for sale to anyone willing to buy without assured title. The mining camps filled and emptied with the seasons and disappeared altogether as new strikes were raised. What could be a booming camp one day might well be a pile of excavated spoil and garbage in two month's time. If a person came to California for any other reason than making money they had arrived in the wrong place.

Many found out just how wrong a place could be in California. One out of six new arrivals would be dead within a year of first getting fitted out in the new golden Eden. Death from dysentery, cholera, or a host of other maladies competed with starvation, drowning, falling, being shot, hung, or being buried alive.

Some camps like Sutter's Fort endured. Not because they were pleasant places to live but because they served as supply depots and jumping off places to the rugged hills, canyons, and arroyos descending from the Sierras. The snowmelt washed the color down from unknown lodes of gold into raging cataracts and pools where the miners plied their skills as soon as the winter runoff subsided enough to work. When winter came, the prospectors retreated to those jumping off places to await a new season. Those lucky enough to have found paydirt would often leave hardship behind and depart for home and local fame as one who "struck it rich in Alta California."

Three years had gone by since Josh first arrived at Sutter's. Other than a few more permanent buildings outside the fort, little had changed. Sutter's was the one place in Gold Country that everyone eventually arrived at. The noise and commerce was enough to give the impression they were all here at once. There were people Josh needed to look up so he left his friends, asking them to wait at the end of town for him.

Josh and Elizabeth had bought a heavy freight wagon from Earl Teague, a teamster who lost his lower leg to an accident and the subsequent infection. As part of the price of the wagon, the young couple promised Teague they would pack him in salt and send his remains back east to his family. So far the skinner survived his ordeal. Josh sought out the trading tent of Stephen Collier and Associates, Teague's employer. Collier was absent but his former employee, now partner, Lewis Werther, was adding new wares to the several chalkboards adorning the canvas storefront and the piles of goods scattered about. The two men shook hands then Josh was swallowed in a bear hug. Werther might be a storekeeper now but he still had the build of a teamster. His hands, big as a bison steak, pummeled his back. Josh inquired about Collier.

"Stephen gets up here now and again just to make certain I'm not robbing him. He's in San Francisco and set up a company bringing in people and goods from Hawaii, China, South America, and God knows where else. Doin' right well at it but seems soon as his ship arrives the crew runs off to become gold barons. I'm probably outfitting some of them here right now. How's your pretty wife and the babe?"

"Both as anxious to see me return as I will be to be back. Healthy and hale I'm happy to say. How's you and your wife?"

"I'm doing fine. Peggy finally moved to the Coast. Couldn't stand the goings on here at the fort night and day. I go to San Francisco now and again to make sure Stephen isn't sampling my goods." Werther laughed good-naturedly. "Sutter moved out, you hear? Turned the operation over to his son and retired to his farm up on the Feather. What brings you by?"

"Headed to Hangtown. Make sure my partners ain't robbin' me blind."

The two men chatted for a bit. Josh bought powder, caps, lead, and a brocade vest as a gift for the newly minted Zachary Hammel. Mounting up, he soon caught up to the coach. Hangtown was too far to make before dark so the company pulled into the woods and camped at a clearing they'd discovered. The coach would hide their fire and picketing the horses on either side of the coach would serve as sentries as they rested. They'd sleep in shifts with one man posted under the coach where any approach from the trail could be spotted.

Josh, his partners, and the two wagon men were passing the evening by the campfire. They were enjoying a comfortable silence after supper just looking into the low flames when Thoms spoke:

"Look at all these trees and hardly a one of them worth the time to cut down. The gray pine, like that one there, is good but they are getting scarce. The sycamore and alder get a decent yield but they be hardwood and that means three times as heavy and three times the work. Cottonwood is easy to find but you might as well cut weeds for what its worth. You know I made my money in a sawpit."

"From what I seen, ain't a rich man in the whole state didn't start out as a bootblack or found a fortune in gold by shaking out his rug," said Colton, the coach guard. Quinn, the driver, spit into the fire—noting his concurrence.

"Well, hell. Its pretty much true," said Hammel, taking no offense. "You come to California a Harvard lawyer or a Congressman's son, like as not you be dead, wrapped in a blanket with a bed slat to mark where you is laid."

"Look at the three of us is payin' your wages," said Thoms. "Hammel here was a teamster just like you two. Bonner was a riverboat mechanic, and I was a farmer with cowshit on my boots. Them two got lucky with the gold but not me. Me and my partners took our last dollars and bought a big whipsaw, dug a pit and started sawin' planks from sunup till we was so stiff we could barely get out of the pit. You try pullin' one end of a ten-foot saw standing in a muddy hole while sawdust pours down your neck twelve hours a day. We didn't get lucky or strike paydirt. We worked till our hands bled and our backs sang sonatas. We started out sellin' planks but soon got smart. After we quit sawyering for the day, we started makin' sluice boxes, rockers, long Toms and such to sell to the new arrivals. Sold them fast as we could make them. Placer mining's had its day. Next thing is sinking shafts and that's going to need timber and I aim to be the man who sells it."

"Haw," said Quinn, once more spitting into the fire. "I seen those big timber trees. Some is thicker than any whipsaw I ever seen and even if you could topple it without getting crushed, they ain't no way to cut it up or move it. Might as well try to get a locomotive down a mountain trail. How you gonna start selling big timber when you cain't do nothin' but look at it?"

"I'll do it," answered Thoms. "How I manage is the reason you're drivin' the coach and I'm ridin' in it."

Hammel laughed. "Damn it boy. He's got you there, he surely do."

"You tryin' to say you three bosses is smarter than us two cause you be payin' us wages," spat Colton.

"Now don't get riled up, son," said Hammel. "Thoms is likely smarter'n all of us. Bonner and me, we just got lucky. Well, lucky and willin' to squat up to our balls in freezing water the whole damn day. Lucky and numb, that's us, Josh. Right?"

"It ain't always luck seen me through. Mindin' what's going on around you just as important. Couple years ago, on the same stretch of road we traveled today, I saved my own life and a pair of miners because I was paying attention. I spied a couple of hard looking characters robbing these two miners, brothers they was. One was standing in their cart, covering them while the other was making them strip so they could steal their clothes."

"Is this for real or you makin' up a campfire tale?" said Colton.

Josh leveled his gaze at Compton. "On the way back, I'll show you where they be buried. Now where was I? I was maybe a hundred yards away when I took my Hawken rifle and shot the one in the cart. The ball drove him right out the back of the wagon. I waited for the other feller to step clear of the miners and shot at him with my pistol, but the range was too long. I might of winged him but if so he didn't pay any attention. He must of figured I had a single shot pistol and would have to reload. He charged right at me swingin' that short axe and howlin' like a wild Indian. Course I still had five shots left so when he got to about twenty feet away, I put one in his chest and he just went down on his face and skidded on it."

"Damn," said Thoms. There were no other comments. Josh stood up.

"I'll take first watch. Who takes next? I need to know whose teeth to knock out if no one comes to spell me."

"I'll take second," said Hammel, "ain't got that many teeth left anyway."

Before getting comfortable, Josh crawled under the coach and out the far side. He walked out into the trees to get familiar with the scene and see if he could spy a piece of the trail they had left earlier. Satisfied, he turned back toward camp. The fire was visible under the coach and was reflecting light up into the surrounding trees. He'd hang a tarp from the coach to hide the fire but the flames would have to slack of their own accord to stop illuminating the trees. Once done, he dragged a buffalo robe and a groundsheet out and propped himself up against the rear wheel. As he settled in a trio of freight wagons rumbled by on the trail. At night, safer to travel in numbers.

Three hours later, Hammel crawled up from behind him and blew beer breath at him. Josh moved nearer the fire, wrapping himself in the buffalo robe to take the chill off. Next thing he knew, Thoms was kicking his foot and offering a metal mug of coffee and a biscuit. Josh told him to set them down while he woke up. He put gloves on so he could hold the coffee. Picking up the heavy biscuit unsure whether it was bread or stone. He dunked the stone until it softened. After breakfast he washed his face and tended to the horse. Josh tied off Natchez to the coach and climbed up to his seat, awaiting the others so they could get on the trail to Hangtown.

The routes between settlements were what passed for roads in California. It was only the passage of iron-tired wheel and shod hoof that distinguished them from native land. They were dust in the summer and sucking mud in the winter. The trail veered around rocks too big to bounce over and smashed the roots of all but the largest trees. All day four and six team freight wagons rumbled along, using their size and momentum to assert their right of way over everything else. The coach would have to pull almost under trees as they met oncoming traffic. From behind, the wagons would only grudgingly surrender scant inches as they pushed past, acknowledging other riders and coaches only with a curse at the lesser folk who dared travel the same route as the lordly teamster.

A coach-and-four, with less weight and better teams, could normally outpace the loaded freight wagons but not on these routes. Bouncing over rocks and roots would soon destroy the coach and batter both team and passenger to animal wreckage. Passengers would often dismount and walk ahead through difficult sections. Eventually, road improvements would come from frustrated passengers who would pry loose an offending boulder and fill the hole with dirt. The teamsters, regular users of the road, would show their gratitude by showering the Samaritan pedestrians with mud or enveloping them in a cloud of dust and grit, dependent up the season.

Those who lived in the gold camps cursed the muleskinners on the road and cursed them again in the camp for the scandalous prices they imposed for the necessities of life delivered. As a result the freighters became a fraternity unto themselves. Damned and cursed by mere mortals, they rode the high boards of the big wagons, as aloof as the captain of a ship at sea. The freight wagons were lords of the road between camps, barely restraining their impulse to grind lesser men under their wheels.

For two days, Josh and his companions endured the muleskinners rumbling abuse and suffered the trail to Hangtown as it climbed into the foothills east of Sutter's. They soon began to encounter scattered clusters of miners, still in winter camp awaiting the cataracts of the American River to subside enough to commence the short season of mining in the hills and canyons. The melting snow would carry the color down from the peaks and leave it in the rivers, creeks, and streams below. The individual prospectors or the small groups of partners had eked out a subsistence winter, panning accessible streams or working for day wages when they could find work.

One of the places these transient prospectors could find work was in the dry diggings, so called because the ore was dug out of embankments far from the streams where it was washed. Josh was one of the pioneers in the dry diggings and owned a one-third share in the first company to work dry. It was to this company's base the coach swung right before crossing the American River into Hangtown. Josh was riding trail again. Thoms complained when Josh caught up.

"Zach and I wanted to be dropped off at the bridge so's we could go into town for a little hoorah."

"The fewer folk see the coach the better I feel. We'll get you to town soon enough but with some escorts to keep you out of trouble."

"It ain't like the two of us is courtin' with maiden aunt Mabel in tow," said Hammel. "Trouble is what we're lookin' for."

"You drink at the wrong place or lie down in the wrong crib and you'll get more grief than you bargain for. You two are one of the few men with a full poke of gold in this camp. There's plenty desperate men here would open your belly and leave you face down in the muck. Our company men know this place and have seen all the scoundrels that ain't yet been hanged or branded."

"He's right, Zach," said Thoms. " I want to gamble and drink and whore without having to have eyes in the back of my head." As if on cue, a chorus of voices rose in cheer across the river. A volley of gunfire punctuated the revelry.

It wasn't like Hangtown or any of the mining camps were without some sense of law and order. Men who had walked across half a continent or spent months on a ship to get to The Promised Land weren't about to become a sheriff and sit in a jail while others made their fortunes in the hills and streams. From the prostitutes in the tents behind the saloons to the hardware merchants to the miners themselves, the business of Alta California was gold. There was no interest in jails and municipal codes or permanent jurists. That didn't mean anything goes.

When scoundrels robbed or killed or when drunken exchanges at the poker table ended in gunfire, justice was meted out on the spot. A Miners' Court was convened, judge and counsel chosen and a jury selected. The evidence was heard, a judgment rendered. If guilt were determined, sentence was passed and executed within the hour. A gambler cheating at cards or a man who steals new boots would be fined or banished from camp. If the offense was serious or habitual, the criminal might be branded with a fireplace poker, leaving a smoking letter "C" or "T" on the cheek. Theft of gold, jumping a claim, or taking a life had more serious consequences. If anything other than self-defense was the verdict and there was some mitigating circumstance to a life-taking the guilty party might face a firing squad. Common killers were hung on the spot. Hanging was more common because a firing squad left a body to be buried. A man hanged could be left as an object lesson for others and the court and counsel could retire to a bar for several rounds of drinks to celebrate a civic duty fulfilled. The pursuit of gold had been momentarily interrupted but law, order and the camp's reputation preserved.

The coach followed a cleared trail parallel to the South Fork of the American River to the site where the mining company washed the ore excavated from the pits and banks above the river. The spoil from each bucket washed was distributed on the ground nearby, eventually building a gravel wash site and wagon turnaround. A right turn from the wash site followed a gravel road inland to the dry diggings.

Josh Bonner and his company of Argonauts from Albany, New York owned the mining rights to some of the richest and largest claims in the region. So far the Company had worked nearly a thousand feet of old bed set back from the American River almost a quarter-mile on a shelf a hundred feet above the wash site. The Albany Company's camp was strung out over the length of their claim. The coach came to a rest by the original cookhouse tents and bunks. The two Albany Company officers were expecting the coach and stepped from the dining tent as the coach rattled to a halt and the passengers stepped down. Josh dismounted his horse and shook hands with his business partners. Thoms and Hammel headed toward the guest bunks to wait.

The officers of the Company had diminished by one, a man with political aspiration back east had sold out to the other partners. Over the past two years, Jack Luders had emerged as the leader of the company when it came to personnel. Fellowes was the acknowledged master at supplies and transportation.

"We've eight hundred and sixty-two ounces since last you were here," informed Luders. "That's here and Bright Hope combined."

"Hell, that's the best yield since last summer."

"There would have been more but we had expenses. We paid wages out, got a lot done," added Fellowes.

"Seen there was just the one long tom working as I come by," said Josh.

"We find pockets as we dig but this placer gold ain't going to last," said Luders.

Fellowes chimed in. "Ain't like there isn't gold to be had. We've uncovered quite a few quartz veins. Some you can dig the color out with a spoon. The rest has to be dug out of the rock and that means crushing rock with pick and hammer. Even then, we can't follow the seam into the hillside more'n three or four feet. Anything more might bring down the whole bluff on our heads."

"What Elias is saying is we can't go into the hill without sinking a shaft. We can't sink a shaft without shoring as we go. We're not that kind of miner. Our boys are farmers and hardware clerks and such. If we want to chase quartz we need to bring real miners. Coal folk or even those Mexican miners from the Southern Diggings. I hear there's even some Cornishmen from England workin' in the south, Quartz Mountain and Grub Gulch."

"We recruit down there and we'll have John Fremont and his syndicate crawling all over the South Fork. Zach Hammel's got a small stamp mill and shaft operation up Pilot Hill. We're headed there and I'll ask him about how his operation works."

"Why not show him what we're up against?" asked Fellowes.

"Hell no. Hammel or Thoms, either see our quartz seams and they'll have a company formed and funded before we get back to San Francisco."

"There's some Carolina fellas round here know about shaft mining. Hear they are puttin' an outfit together for when the river drops," said Fellowes.

"I say, let'em go up river," Luders added. "Once they get tired of freezin' their butts and fingers for an ounce a day, we'll offer good wages, a bunk, and chow."

"We're lucky here. We can work year 'round," said Fellowes. "Biggest problem is keeping the men on this side of the river so they don't drink and screw themselves broke every night in Hangtown."

"Hey, speaking of Hangtown," said Josh. "You got a couple dependable men who can take care of themselves and mind Garrett and Zach in town? They got their minds fixed on a whiskey hoorah and a tour of the finer bordellos in town. I'll pay good men to bring those two back under their own power."

"Zach Hammel wants to get his carrot wet," laughed Jack Luders. "That flea hotel couldn't get into a whorehouse with a fistful of Liberty Head eagles."

"He's changed since last you saw him. We cleaned him up for the trip and I think he's started usin' lavender tonic. You got a couple boys want to make an ounce of flake for the night's work and won't drink it up on the job?"

"We'll fix you up with a couple serious men ain't so grim the sight of a whore's crib won't give them the vapors."

"Then let's get my friends over here for a shot or two of the good stuff, send them on their way. Then we can talk business."

###

Josh rose early to supervise the packing of the gold shipment into the strongbox. Seven leather-wrapped whiskey bottles were corked, sealed with wax and laid in the strong box in a bed of pine needles. With the help of the two company officers, the job was completed before the camp began to stir. Certainly before Thoms and Hammel arose. With the assistance of the two escorts, they returned safely, if lighter in the purse, from their carouse. The celebrants arose after cook quit serving breakfast, making the way from bunk to chow tent with squinting eyes and unsteady gait. They managed to reheat some fried potatoes and wash them down with coffee strong enough to bring back the shine on a rusted nail. Attempts at conversation were greeted with a scowl and a mumbled flurry of curses. Josh was thankful he'd never acquired a taste for John Barleycorn.

When it was time to depart, Josh volunteered to ride horseback as the backtrail, spelling Thoms and allowing his companions to find what peace they could in the rattling coach. Thoms grunted something that might have been a thank you as he managed to draw down the window shades before curling up on the rear bench of the coach. Josh was saying his goodbyes as the driver urged the team down the gravel road. He was getting ready to mount up when Fellowes approached with two mounted men, the escorts from last night.

"Finley and Grant," said Fellowes, with a nod indicating the two riders, "said your friends was splashing their money around pretty free last night. A few rough-looking fellers was pretending hard not to notice. Our boys didn't hear your friends say anything about their plans or where they was from but couldn't keep an eye on them while they was passin' time with the ladies.

Could of drawn the girls a map for all either of ours could tell."

"They must've got talked our last night. Neither had ten words to say this morning."

"Liquor has that effect on some men. Anyways, I'm going to send these two with you at least part of the way out of Hangtown."

Both are dependable and will back your play if you have to make one. Josh shook hands all around. Josh recalled meeting both at some time in the past and recognized them as partners in The Greater Albany Company and not men working for wages. The company had had its ups and downs over the past three years. Men came and went but these men stayed and Fellowes vouched for them, Josh figured they could be counted upon. The trio stood to their saddles and cantered along until they figured to be a mile or less behind the coach. A few freight wagons blundered past them, crowding them just so the skinner could say he'd done so, but no mounted men were spotted. The morning passed without event. Finley produced some jerky for lunch, pungent with Mexican spices, some biscuits still retaining warmth from the cloth they were wrapped in and a small milk can of the morning's coffee— still just as strong but barely drinkable cold. The trio rode along, content in the tranquil sounds of nature and the creaking of their saddle leather and the occasional opinion from a horse.

When the first shots rang out, they might have been forgiven their initial confusion. The hills disguised the direction but only for a moment.

"Son of a bitches ran on ahead of use last night," growled Finley. Finley and Grant spurred ahead together. Josh was only a moment behind but, being better mounted, overtook them in but a few long strides.

The shooting continued but not in the fusillade a person might expect at a coach robbery with all the players armed to the teeth. They listened as they galloped along. The shots were interspersed. One or two would ring out, another would answer. Then it would be quiet for a bit and then another one or two shots more. The hillsides carried the echoes but it seemed the exchange was moving off the road up into one of the draws.

They caught sight of the coach through the trees for just a moment then rounded a bend to find the coach halted by the verge of the trail. Colton, the guard was on top of the coach, providing both a better view and simultaneously a handsome target. Hammel and Thoms were dismounted, guns in both hands, and looking for trouble. Both started to raise their pistols toward the new arrivals before instantly recognizing them as friends. The three riders reined up hard, the horses' rumps sinking as the hooves dug in.

Thoms saved Josh from asking.

"Damnedest thing. Two men come poundin' down the road. Heard them long before they arrived. Took one look at us and turned up that wash," pointing to a gap in the trees on the right. Hammel walked up, guns holstered and continued the story.

"Two three minutes goes by and half a dozen men, lathered up bad as their horses, come up on us from the same direction. They don't say a word but just look us over. We point where the other fellers went and off they went. Couple minutes more and that skirmish you hear breaks out."

Together they listened for the intermittent gunshot.

"Somethin's got t'happen," said Finley. "That arroyo only goes up 'bout three-quarter mile. Ends in a pool under a bluff. Think the pool is fed by a spring that feeds the creek there. Been panned out for a long time. Nice enough place to sit by the pool and have a lunch and smoke."

A couple minutes more went by in silence, then a dozen or more shots filled the air quicker than could be counted, then silence.

"Think we should ride up and take a look?" said Grant.

"Hell no we shouldn't," said Hammel, giving the man a look like he'd just exposed a fool. "Whosomever's still alive up there's got their blood up. You go prancin' up that wash, you'll come sprinting back, if you're able to ride."

That seemed to settle the question. They waited.

"Ain't no place else to go but back down this way," said Finley, adding, "ain't but three-quarter mile long," in case the gathering had forgotten.

Five more minutes and eight horses emerged single file. Six had riders and two had bodies wrapped in blankets and tied over the saddles. Once they were all back on the trail, two men separated from the group and nudged their mounts slowly toward the coach. When the seven at the coach just casually let their hands drop toward their holsters, the two men raised their hands high as their elbows and displayed empty palms. Thoms nodded them forward.

One of them, a big-shouldered stocky man spoke. He wasn't the kind to wait for questions before answering the obvious.

"Them two", pointing back over his shoulder, "went on a killin' and robbin' spree yesterday up above Poverty Bar on Kennebec Creek. Kilt and robbed John Beasley and his wife in their tent. Then another miner right at his campfire eatin' breakfast."

He turned to his companion as if to ask the wife's name or the lone miner. His partner shrugged his ignorance.

"They was three of them when they left the Kennebec. Robbed a man ridin' on the road. He dropped one of them before they hit him. He's back the road aways—expect he'll live."

"Thanks to you for bringin' out the remains," said Hammel. "Understand there's a pool and spring up there be a nice place for a man to spend an afternoon. Wouldn't want to picnic up there and find the spring poisoned with some galoot's body."

"I'll take your word on the scenery. Our minds was elsewhere."

"You know who these fellers were?" asked Josh.

"No idea who they was or why they went crazy. We just couldn't abide what they was doin' so we lit out and settled their hash."

"Still decent of you to see them buried."

"Just the saddle on the gray will cover buryin' the three of them with enough left over for a preacher and a marching band if we was inclined, which we ain't."

The man who shrugged decided it was time to speak.

"We ain't man hunters. Ya just can't let shit like what happened go by. Besides, the wounded man will need doctorin' and the dead should be buried proper and their families' tolt of what happened."

"Well, that's all the tellin of it. You men look like you have better things to do than jabber in the thoroughfare." The pair swung around and rejoined their group. They bunched up and rode away.

"Didn't catch their names now, did we?" said Josh.

"Where's they say they was from?" asked Thoms.

"Poverty Bar on Kennebec Creek," answered Hammel.

"Ain't heard of neither of them but I'm of a mind to keep it that way," said Grant. It was enough of a joke to get a laugh and break the tension before they all mounted up and prepared to roll.

The party spent the night at the same camp they used on the trip to Hangtown. No one admitted to being shaken by the day's events but none voiced an objection to making a cold camp. A small fire was lit in the morning for coffee, reheated biscuits, and fried ham. Finley and Grant, with few words, split from their companions and rode back home. Both men impressed him with their resolve. He tucked their names into his head for future reference. Two hours travel dodging freighters coming from both directions and they reached the intersection where the trail from Hangtown to Auburn camp met the road to Sacramento. Making their way alongside the Middle Fork of the American River on their left they kept on toward Auburn camp.

Josh had mixed feelings about this reach of the American. It was upstream from the river on a creek now known as the Humbug. Josh and Elizabeth had first dipped a pan and learned how to "twirl" it to wash the color from the tailings. Further up the Humbug they had discovered a sheer bluffed box canyon where they pried ribbons of gold loose from the rock with sharpened spoons. The entry was difficult—the mouth blocked with scree and toppled dead timber. Circumstances interfered and no claim was ever filed. Every time he passed the creek mouth he was tempted to go see if anyone had discovered his find.

Auburn camp, the next destination, had no such pleasant memories. Josh and his wife had both lost their families to cholera. They'd arrived at Auburn to find there was a cholera outbreak eating through the settlement. Auburn was seemingly cursed with periodic outbreaks of pestilence. Cholera, dysentery, smallpox, and tales of bad luck were regular news from Auburn. Destruction seemed drawn there like fortune hunters to California. Some called it Sutter's curse as it was near here Sutter started to build a sawmill to harvest and mill the trees floated down to the mill. Instead, gold had been raised and within a year, the mill was abandoned and Sutter's *rancho*, his New Helvetica townsite, his fort and all his holdings had been overrun and plundered by gold seekers. Nowadays Sutter was rumored to be a recluse, drowning himself in brandy.

The coach detoured up the Middle Fork toward two claims of Zach Hammel's. The middle fork was famous for rich bars where the turns in the river dropped deposits of gold. Outposts like Mormon Bar, Horseshoe Bar, and Gold Hill became names spoken across the nation. There were hundreds of sandbars but only a handful raised enough color to make the owner wealthy

Zachary Hammel had, like almost all the soldiers in California, deserted his post in Monterey to seek his fortune. No officers or sergeants were going to come arrest him. They were all working shoulder to shoulder beside him.

They halted at the top of a small hill. As the river narrowed it was not possible to drive a coach up the river. Hammel mounted up and made his way alone upstream. The rest of the crew made camp. The hilltop location meant they could not be approached unseen. They watched the rump of Hammel's horse until he was out of sight.

"He figures it's safer for one man who looks like a busted miner than bringin' an army upstream," said Thoms.

"This outfit is hardly an army and now he's cleaned himself up, his partners won't know who he is," said Josh.

"I wonder who his partners are."

"Never mentioned names. Just some prospectors he used to sell supplies to and then grubstaked is what he says."

"Always been tight lipped till the liquor passes them."

Josh felt Thoms was trying to get him to loosen up about his own operation. How much Josh pulled out and was now in the coach strong box was none of Thoms' business. Rather than insult the man, Josh made busy setting up camp. This spot was where they stopped every time they awaited Hammel's return. They'd killed rattlesnakes here before and it was getting warm enough they might be about. From long habit Josh laid out a rope around where he was going to sleep. The practice always amused his traveling companions. He had no proof the rope kept the snakes away but he slept easier because of it. After supper and some jabber around the fire, they turned in. The others, Josh noted, all slept on or in the coach.

Their temporary bivouac, besides being situated with its view, was a peaceful place compared to the other nights spent on the road. There was no advantage to the traders to drive up the river. Their customers would come down to them where the main trail forded the river. The miners, wary of poor footing along the banks, wouldn't venture down after dark. A man could lie under the stars and enjoy the solitude and the burbling of the current.

Hammel returned by lunchtime, looking no different than when he left. As was the custom, Hammel mounted the stage, pulled the curtains and made his deposit to the strong box. A man's wealth was his own private business. The coach rolled down the hill, followed the current and rejoined the parade of travelers and freight wagons on the road to Auburn camp.

Auburn Camp was swarming with veterans and newcomers setting up rockers and sluice boxes on both banks. Oftentimes the final wash would reveal a fifty- dollar pan to the exclamations of those who held it. No on ran over to examine the wonder. There might be just such a pan in their claims. It could be the next pan. The whoops and laughter probably encouraged the pace of those endeavors. No one paid any attention to a dusty coach crossing the ford and heading through the camp upstream on the North Fork.

Auburn Camp was set quite a ways back from the rivers. There was a single muddy main street and several side paths dictated primarily by topography. Every enterprise connected with the collection or spending of gold could be found within a quarter-mile walk. Each time Josh and his friends arrived there seemed to be a few more permanent buildings replacing the original tent city. It was rumored a doctor and some other residents who had faith in the camp's permanence had built houses and offices of brick but they saw none as they passed through and left the hub-bub behind. They were headed for Forest Hill where Thoms had a syndicate of men working a cutbank near the river. They would collapse part of the bank, looking for the black sand and then wash what they could. The sandbar they staked the claim on was played out but the ore from the bluff was still worth working. They stopped for about an hour while Thoms collected the washout gold, collected mail and a list of provisions to have sent up. Thoms wasn't shy about his wealth and didn't ask his companions to step down while he deposited a saddlebag in the strong box.

Beyond Forest Hill the North Fork began the grade into the Sierras. Where Blue Lead Creek had its confluence with the American, there was a ford. The coach crossed the ford and commenced climbing again. Several times the passengers and the guard dismounted and walked to ease the burden on the team. Eventually they came to a broad, level meadow between two looming foothills. Blue Lead ran right through the meadow from its source between the hills. Josh and Thoms had staked this venture with a syndicate of eight other Argonauts. Each man staked a claim under the local mining rules and no other persons could work the creek from the meadow to the rubble pile at the source. Because the creek was sourced from several freshets and the meadow had such a gradual fall, the sandbars could be worked nearly year round. The claim wouldn't pay forever but while it did, the Blue Lead Mine pulled up pans of color of the kind that made people in New Hampshire, Delaware, and Alabama pick up stakes and make their way to The Promised Land.

The men had raised just under four hundred and thirty ounces of dust and flake and a dozen ounces of nugget gold. After the raw gold was smelted to nearly pure and expenses had been deducted, each member of the syndicate would have earned about five hundred dollars for the month. Back East wages ranged from a dollar to a dollar and a half for a ten to twelve hour day. For a month's misery in the diggings, the men accumulated what a family farm could accumulate in a generation. The Blue Lead was a claim worth protecting. These men didn't work more than an arm's reach from their weapons. They didn't venture down to Auburn Camp for leisure pursuits come Sunday. If they had, they would likely return to a hundred men spread over their meadow bawling and fighting for their share.

The arrival of the partners occasioned a little respite from the labors. In anticipation of the managers' arrival a deer had been shot and butchered. Thoms had brought some delicacies from below. Champagne bottles chilled in the stream. Canned condensed milk and brandy was mixed in enamel cups and three sacks of lemons and oranges were distributed like party favors. The venison was roasted, the sparkling wine was swilled like water in the same enameled cups, and the men relaxed around the red coals of the cook fire. Soon they all retired, contented. Men rubbed their bellies to remind themselves of the evening's consumption. The morning would come and there was tons of sand yet to sluice and wash.

In the canyons and arroyos of gold country, dawn did not arrive early. Sunlight had to scale the Sierras and many of the canyons, like Blue Lead included, lay between foothills. The men rose, not with the sun but with the routine of their labors. They would work most of their day in a half-light.

The three partners, the driver, and guard rose in the stingy light of the new day's arrival. They tended to their stock, readied the coach, and scrubbed away the sleep in the icy water. They didn't consult their watches. They weren't meeting a train or answering a factory whistle. The road they traveled was demanding enough in sunlight. They would wait. They ate breakfast and drank their coffee. Thoms had secreted a little brandy. He poured a dollop in his cup, offering it around. The syndicate men declined, hesitant to imbibe in front of the bosses on a workday morn. Josh declined, shaking his head at the offer. Zach Hammel stuck out his cup. Colton and Quinn were getting ready for departure and not part of the offer. They watched but didn't seem to take any offense at the exclusion. They were working for wages and expected nothing more than their due. When Hammel looked their way they nodded they were ready to roll.

"Time to ride, boys," he said after tipping the last of the brandied coffee down his throat. "Or in your cases, time to bounce around. My turn to ride today. Your turn to get your teeth loosened."

"We're lettin' you ride, old man, cause you ain't got the teeth to spare," said Josh.

"That's a good one," laughed Thoms as he disappeared into the coach and claiming the forward facing seat. "I'm gonna borrow it if you don't mind."

The driver and guard were already in the box when Josh looked around the camp. It was a workday and no one was going to come see them off. A couple of men working the long tom waved. Josh raised a hand in reply as he closed the door.

"I'm laggin' behind a few minutes and can say your goodbyes for ya. Anyone special I should give a hug and a kiss?" said Hammel. It was payback for Josh's earlier jibe. The road was going to be dusty. He dropped the side curtains all around.

"Thanks," said Thoms. "The dark is a comfort to my fuzzy head." He pulled his slouch hat down as if he were on a saloon porch, ready for a snooze. It was a signal he wasn't interested in conversation. Quinn yapped at the horses, cracked the reins over their backs and urged them on.

###

They reached the descent from the meadow and started down. Both Quinn and Colton were working the footbrakes and the smell of hot leather permeated the close atmosphere inside. The pace quickened but the passengers weren't concerned. From the descent they tell Quinn was a competent driver. Josh speculated on the pace of their journey. If they made good time, got through Auburn Camp quickly and only stopped for a quick noon meal, it still meant the last piece before arriving at The Landing would be after dark. He was speculating whether it was more dangerous to make camp in their regular spot past the junction or to risk carrying a fortune in gold down a road growing almost legendary for its robberies. When they reached the ford, crossed and turned right for Auburn Camp, Josh raised the curtain on his right side. Riding backwards downhill was making him queasy. The fresh air and being able to see what passed by would help.

They had no sooner passed the first long turn in the road when Josh felt the team and coach lurch to the left. The commotion approaching could only mean a freight wagon was asserting its right to half the road but taking it in the middle.

They kept moving left until he felt the iron tires touch the rock scree at the bottom of a steep bluff. The coach tipped, not much but enough to warrant grabbing the sill. The imbalance roused Thoms who peeled off his hat.

"What the hell?" he started to say but was cut off by the voices of Quinn and Colton cursing the teamster. The front hub of the coach scraped dirt from the bluff as the coach came to a quick halt. They could hear the harness and hooves of the freighter's team as it passed their darkened windows. Then the team halted. Their driver and guard could be heard clearly, inventing new names for the muleskinner and his family heritage. Never one to pass up a verbal hoo-rah, Thoms rolled up the leather curtain and stuck his head out and began to chime in with the tirade. He'd just opened his mouth for a volley when the roar and blast of a shotgun took Thoms in the chest and he toppled backwards over the strongbox. Where he had been standing Josh saw only the high gray boards of the freight wagon. He saw movement between the boards.

In the second it took for Josh to take all this in, a rifle chimed in and Colton's voice was silenced. Josh could hear the sound of is body slumping into the box and his shotgun clattering to its floor. The nightmare they all feared but didn't talk about had arrived.

Josh slid to the floor and grabbed the door handle, putting his shoulder to it as the latch released. If he didn't get out of the coach he was going to be dead in a few breaths. The door slammed up against the bluff. Josh looked at the gap. It looked big enough a frightened man might wiggle through it but he'd be helpless if he tried and he'd be shot to pieces hanging upside down, a fate he couldn't bear to consider. He pulled the buffalo robe over the seat and threw it over his body. The robe would disguise his shape to whoever came to finish him. He dragged Thoms down over him.

Thoms was still alive, but barely so. His chest was a mess and he was breathing ragged and shallow as blood bubbled out his mouth and down his cheek. Josh had an impression of the contrast of blood on white teeth. Thoms' face wasn't a foot from Josh's. He was looking directly into Josh's eyes but he wasn't seeing anything. There was life for a moment before Josh felt his last breath speckle his skin with blood.

Josh loosened the strap behind the hammer of his holstered Walker Colt and pulled the weapon free. He always kept all six chambers charged and capped, relying on the restraining strap to prevent inadvertent discharge. From this point on, every shot had to have purpose.

There was movement behind the wagon's boards. The wagon was tight up against the coach. The position and the height of the freighter's boards was all the slim protection Josh enjoyed. Firing into the coach over the boards was at such a steep angle, bullets couldn't reach his side of the coach. Josh curled up behind the strong box and under his friend's body as hands with pistols in them appeared over the top of the board as the enemy tested the theory. The charge from a shotgun tried out the floor of the coach for durability.

As soon as the volley ended a hand rose over the windowsill and started firing. The brown crown of a hat with a feather in it could be seen over the sill top. What was he thinking, Josh thought. The man had concealment but he didn't have any cover. The coach side wasn't even half an inch thick. Josh put a .44 caliber ball through the door about eight inches below the crown of the hat. The hat disappeared followed by the hand and arm. The pistol clattered to the floor.

From outside came a pistol shot that thunked into the freight wagon.

"Get than son of a bitch, Mel," came a voice, reedy with a mix of anger, excitement, and fear. "And don't hit those horses."

"The bastards dancin' around behind the horses," replied another. "Why don't you jump down and circle around t'other side?"

"Come on, fellas, I'm waitin' for ya," came the raspy voice of Quinn. The words were bravado but the voice was all fear.

One thing was certain. Before too long the gang of robbers, minus one, would be coming for both driver and passenger. They probably would just stand in the driver's box and shoot down through the roof or come up behind and blast away through the boot. Josh had to do something and it didn't take but a moment for him to realize the boot was his escape.

The boot was a shelf on the rear of the coach made to carry extra luggage or parcels. Two pieces of oiled canvas protected the boot from the shelf to the top rear of the coach body. The boot, Josh knew was accessible from inside the coach. Josh took a quick peek for movement in the wagon and jumped from his shelter. He slipped the two buckles on the seatback so it dropped forward. In two quick steps he was crouched in the boot, peeking out between the seam of the canvas halves.

He didn't have to wait long. A pocked-face man with stringy hair came into view. He held his pistol out before him. As the face entered his field, Josh stuck the barrel of his pistol into the crack. The man sensed the movement but before he could react Josh had put a ball in his ear. Listening for a man on the roof and hearing nothing but willing to risk all. Josh parted the canvas and jumped down, landing in a crouch. He looked up, expecting to be shot for his troubles but there was nothing but sky and bluff face. He turned toward the wagon.

He could see the thighs and legs of a man by the front wheel. It was a tough shot but Josh took it anyway. He saw white wood and knew he's hit a spoke as the man yelped and fell to the ground, struck by the ball or a splinter. Josh pulled back the hammer and aimed to finish him.

Before he could fire a rifle cracked from nearly above his head. Josh hugged the coach body to keep from exposing himself. Was there someone on top? He'd be easy pickings.

"I'm hit, boys. I'm hit bad--." The last word faded into a gurgle. It seemed to come from the wagon box. Josh could still see some movement between the boards.

"Finish him, Josh," came Hammel's voice from above. "There ain't but one of 'em left." The words were followed by a flurry of pistol shots that peppered the wagon.

Josh, ignoring the man with the wounded foot, stepped to the back of the wagon to find a man crouched with a shotgun, cowering in the corner. Josh put two shots into his body and he slumped even lower, relaxed in death. One shot left, Josh thought. He stepped around the rear of the wagon to deal with the man he'd wounded. The man's weapon was in the dirt by the front wheel. He was moaning about his wounded ankle that was leaking pretty well. He froze and looked at his captor when Josh told him to quit moving and put his hands out where he could see.

"That's it. We've done for 'em. You can come out now, Quinn." Josh looked up and there was Zach Hammel, thirty feet above him on the top of the bluff.

"Well, finally. Here come the boys from camp. Hope we didn't interrupt their breakfast."

Hammel pointed his empty rifle back up the road. "I'm comin' down. Don't shoot me."

All the men from the syndicate were mounted. A variety of weaponry was on display. They saw the show was over and slowed to a trot.

"We got your horse back, Josh," came a voice from the crowd. "Looks like he broke his tether when it got noisy." Josh hadn't even noticed Natchez was missing. The riders dismounted and held the reins of their mount. Quinn emerged from behind the wagon team where he'd sheltered. Hammel came up the road. Together they paused by the coach's trees where Colton's body lay crumpled in the dust. There was already a skim of dust on his clothes and on the spillage on the ground.

"God Damn it to Hell!" cried Quinn. "I partnered with Jim two years now. The bastards didn't say a word. Bastard just popped up from the wagon bed and drilled him. I bailed off the box but nothin' I could do. Jim's shotgun fell in the wagon box." The usually grim driver put his face in his arms and sobbed against the coach.

"Anyone else hurt. Where's Garrett?" asked Hammel.

"Dead. Shotgunned from three feet. He's in the coach."

"This the one?" One of the syndicate boys pointed a cocked pistol at the wounded man.

"Nope," said Josh. "One with a scattergun's in the wagon."

"Don't make no difference," said another miner. While Josh and Garrett Thoms were the managers of the Blue Lead claim, it was Thoms who had been with them from the beginning. Josh had only backed their stake when approached by Garrett.

One of the miners seized the wounded man by his collar. Another by his belt and dragged him to the other verge of the trail.

"Take pity, fellas," the man begged, knowing there was none to be found. One of the miners kicked him in his wounded ankle. He howled in pain. The miners stood by his feet, waiting until he stopped his caterwauling. Then, in a ragged volley, they shot him near to pieces. Josh and Hammel watched. Quinn was trying to get himself together. Hammel shrugged his indifference to the summary execution.

"Saves havin' to hang him."

"I thought I was done for when I heard the rifle shot from above me. Glad it was you," said Josh. The miners, after reloading, gathered around the managers. One of them put his arm around Quinn, consoling him. Hammel had the stage.

"I was a ways back but I seen that wagon comin' up the road and just thought it was another rude teamster till I heard the shootin'. I was right at the toe of the slope of that bluff and figured the top would be a good place for me to be. By the time I got dismounted and ready to fire, you had things pretty much in hand."

"The hell. I didn't know where but one of them was and didn't know how many there were. My hands is still shakin'".

"I shot the one was stalkin' Quinn. When I realized he didn't want to hurt the team, I kind of figured what their plan was."

Nobody had to ask to get Hammel to go on. They knew him well enough.

"Figured they needed the coach because they couldn't take the time to get into the strong box or pry it away. They planned on taking the coach. Then they was going to drive the freighter up and block the way down out of the meadow, shoot the horses and take off to wherever they planned to meet. No idea where that might've been and now we can't ask anyone," he finished, nodding toward the bandit in the road.

Jim Colton's body was retrieved from under the coach. With reverence the miners removed remains of Garrett Thoms from the coach body. They used the dead men's bedrolls to wrap them in. Needle and twine were produced and the blankets sewn into shrouds. Both were a little short and their boots stuck out. They wrapped twine around their ankles so the legs wouldn't flop about and prepared to lift them to the top of the coach.

"No," said Josh. "Put them inside the coach. We roll into Auburn with two bodies on the roof and it will draw every layabout in camp. We'll just pass through quiet like."

The bodies of their friends were placed in the coach. One on each side of the strong box. Their legs were folded to fit around the box they'd died trying to protect. A man produced a pocket Bible and read a verse about there being a time for everything. Then he led a recitation of the Lord's Prayer and there was nothing more to be done for them.

The bodies of the five robbers were tossed up into the bed of the freight wagon and laid out two on top of three. Zach Hammel barked a short laugh.

"Last night these skunks was sittin' round their fire, planning their action and went to bed spending their share of the gold in their dreams. Now they're all dead and fixin' to be dumped in a single grave with a plank of wood carved, Five Robbers and the date."

He turned to Josh who had mounted the coach driver's box, shotgun at the ready. Quinn had collected himself and held the reins, waiting for the order to move.

"You go on ahead and roll through Auburn Camp. I'll wait a bit then deliver this rotting meat down below. These boys will follow me so no one thinks I'm takin' all the credit and to answer any questions about what happened. Half-hour from now no one will remember a coach even passed by. We'll meet up at the bivouac past the junction." Josh nodded. The coach rolled out with Natchez tethered behind.

At Auburn camp, no one paid any attention to the coach except a freighter who felt they were holding him up. They arrived at their usual rest by late afternoon.

"I don't know if Thoms has any people I should tell," said Josh.

"Jim has a brother works for a chandler at Sutter's," said Quinn. "Jesus, I can't let him see him like this."

Quinn dug out a change of clothing for his friend, stripped off the bloody garments and soaked them to use to scrub away the dried blood. Josh, because it now seemed wrong not to do it, performed the same ablutions for Thoms.

Meanwhile, at Auburn Camp, Zach Hammel drove the shot-up freight wagon and its cargo of corpses down the main thoroughfare until so many gathered he had to halt. Following him were five of the men from Blue Lead Creek leading the horses they discovered at the robbers' camp off the roadway. Hammel stood up.

"These men tried to jump our claim and kill us all. They're all dead for their troubles and the same will happen to anyone else who tries."

The wagon full of dead men and five grim riders all backing Hammel's story, put to rest any objections from the gathering.

"They used this wagon to come up to our camp. I expect it's stolen and I expect the man who owns it is lyin' dead along the road somewhere. I'm leavin' it here, anyways. You folks figure it out. I'm keepin' these dead men's horses, 'cept for one. Anyone steps up to bury these boys can take their pick."

A man in the crowd spoke up.

"One horse don't quite seem like enough for five men."

"Bury'em all in the same hole. I don't care. If it makes you feel better you can keep the saddle."

Several men stepped up to examine the selection. One fellow, who obviously knew horseflesh, selected a bay gelding. He exchanged glances with Hammel to seal the deal, tipped his hat and walked away with his prize.

It was well after dark and the campfire was a gray ember when Josh heard a horse approaching.

"Coming in. Its Hammel."

"Any trouble in Auburn?" asked Josh.

"I'm here, ain't I?" said Hammel. "As soon as I said they was claim jumpers it was all over. A highwayman ain't no ways hated like a claim jumper. Anything to eat?"

He helped himself to coffee and picked a couple pieces of lukewarm ham from the pan.

"I see you cleaned them up," said Hammel as he chewed. "Thank you for doing that. I don't think I'd have the sand for it."

"It was terrible getting them out of the coach, them stiff and all," said Quinn, who had awakened. "Don't mind saying I was scared the whole time even though it don't make no sense to be scared."

"Did Garrett have any kin?" asked Josh. "I never talked much about family with him."

"He lived with his brother and two Mexican women in a place up top of Russian Hill. I'll tell them when we get him back."

When the morning light came through the trees, they kicked out the remains of the fire and turned toward the road. This time the bodies of their friends rode on top of the stage. There was no sense laying them back on the bloody floor of the coach. Hammel rode the box and Josh rode trail. He encountered several passersby who were speculating with friends about the dead men riding the coach roof they just passed. Josh rode up behind the coach as it turned to go up the hill at Sutter's Landing. A crowd gathered and followed along on foot, calling out questions. Neither Quinn nor Hammel even acknowledged their presence with so much as a glance. A man, insistent on having his questions answered, was so bold as to lay hand on the bridle of the lead horse. Hammel rewarded his boldness with a crack of the whip inches before his eyes. Hammel dug an elbow into Quinn's ribs and chuckled.

"Good to know I ain't lost my skills."

They were welcomed at the Van Volk home with as much enthusiasm as when they first arrived. The mood turned somber as the story unfolded. Quinn was paid sixty dollars for the coach rental and seventy-five dollars each for he and Compton. Josh and Hammel each paid another fifty in bonus, burial and to pay for the damages to the rig. Quinn left on foot to inquire about a coffin. Now they were settled and safe, Hammel finally broke down, shedding tears for his lost friend and blowing his nose repeatedly in his new handkerchief. The Mexican cook who had earlier vandalized his food took pity on him and brought him a towel from the kitchen after he'd used up the kerchief. A person could only guess whether it was because of his emotions or because he looked almost handsome cleaned up in his new outfit.

Quinn returned at dinnertime. Hammel spared Josh the duty and helped Quinn wash out the coach. After breakfast, Josh said his goodbyes to Natchez. Quinn drove them down to the river and westward. Josh rode inside. Hammel sat in the box, occasionally reaching back to pat his departed friend's boot. Passing the glade where they rendezvoused with the coach they went directly to the launch. There was too much gold for two men to carry. Besides, Quinn's trustworthiness was no longer in question. It would be dark before they got to San Francisco. If there were danger afoot, it would come from the banks of the river so they were glad to pass that reach in full daylight.

###

Elizabeth stood at the taffrail of the Essex underneath the two lanterns, one above the other--she'd run up the mizzenmast. This was her second night looking for Josh's launch to cross the reflection of the moon on the bay. She knew she needn't worry. Josh and his companions were all competent men but they were a day overdue and it was only natural for a wife with a young child to fret about her man. She picked up the bottle of Madeira from the deck, filling the glass on the railing by her elbow. She didn't drink it but it was there if she needed.

Josh rowed quietly just offshore passing Washerwoman Cove. He debated saying anything to Elizabeth about the robbery, Garrett Thoms' death, and his role in the affair. She'd sooner throw what gold they had due back into the rivers than let him venture out again. Certainly, he wouldn't say anything tonight and spoil his homecoming. He'd have to tell her soon. The story of the "claim jumpers" would make its way down the trail and she'd hear something from someone. Tomorrow would be a good time. He spotted the two stacked lanterns of his floating home and sprinted across the bay, the lights of San Francisco shining brightly on his left.

Elizabeth felt a bump and instantly knew it was the launch coming up against the hull. She ran to the sideboard and peered over the railing to see Josh finish tying off.

"How did you get past me?" she said. "I've been watching from the back all night"

"The stern. I hugged the shoreline all the way until I saw the signal.

Toss me a line.”

For the next quarter-hour Josh tied off saddlebags filled with leather pokes of gold and filled a basket with golden whiskey bottles while Elizabeth hauled them on deck.

“One more,” he shouted. She hauled it up with a grin. There was a lot of gold.

“Oops. Found another,” he said.

Later, “Oops, one more.”

Finally Josh climbed the ladder, came aboard and hugged his wife. It was good to have gold but it was better to be home.

THE END

If you liked Incident at Blue Lead Creek, you are in luck. It's the first in a series of shorts about Josh and Elizabeth, the early days in San Francisco, Gold Country, and perhaps Zach Hammel. I took a shine to the ornery varmint as I was writing this one.

If you are feeling adventurous there are three full-length novels featuring Josh and Elizabeth Bonner, all available as a kindle edition or as a paperback on Amazon.

<u>The Platte River Waltz, Orphans in the Storm</u> chronicles how Josh and Elizabeth are orphaned by a cholera epidemic as their families emigrate to Oregon Territory in early 1848. Determined to continue, they are adopted by another train from Missouri. Josh is taken under the wing of the French *voyageur* scout and educated in the way of the wilds. Elizabeth's fierce determination carries them through.

<u>The Platte River Waltz, The Growler Brigade</u> picks up the trail at Fort Laramie where the emigrant train learns of the discovery of gold in Alta California. The news divides the train and some wagons split to set course for California. Josh and Elizabeth are now California bound with Josh leading the way. FYI, a growler is the name for a gold nugget as it rattles around in the prospector's pan.

<u>Hangtown</u> continues the young couple's adventures in the wild gold camps of California and the rivers of the Sierras. They partner up with an English mining engineer, Duncan Shipwash, and decide to make their fortunes in a land without government, law, or rules.

I've also written two hard-boiled detective novels in the style of the pulp fiction of the 1930's. I've always been a big fan of Raymond Chandler (The

Big Sleep, Lady in the Lake) and I've tried to be faithful to the style but moved the action south to ritzy Orange County. Try <u>Deadly Talley</u> and <u>Dean's List</u> for a change of pace.

If you like any or all of these offerings, please leave a nice review. To an independent author, a good review is almost as satisfying as any royalties that accrue.

Ken Consaul, August 25, 2017